Amritabindu Upanishad

A Drop of Immortality

Commentary by
Swami Tejomayananda

Central Chinmaya Mission Trust

First Edition – July 2010 to January 2014– 7,000 copies
Second Edition – September 2016 to September 2023 – 6,300 copies
Reprint - April 2025 - 2,500 copies

Published by:
Chinmaya Prakashan
The Publications Division of
Central Chinmaya Mission Trust
Sandeepany Sadhanalaya
Saki Vihar Road, Powai, Mumbai 400072, India
Tel.: +91-22-2803 4900
Email: ccmtpublications@chinmayamission.com
Website: www.chinmayamission.com

Distribution Centre in the USA:
Chinmaya Publications West
560 Bridgetown Pike
Feasterville, PA 19053-7240, USA
Tel.: (215) 396-0390, Fax: (215) 396-9710
Email: publications@chinmayamission.org
Website: www.chinmayapublications.com

Designed by: Chinmaya Kalpanam, Mumbai

Printed by: SAP Print Solutions Pvt. Ltd., Mumbai

ISBN 978-81-7597-485-2

Transliteration and Pronunciation Guide

In this book, Devanagari characters are transliterated according to the scheme adopted by the International Congress of Orientalists at Athens in 1912. In it one fixed pronunciation value is given to each letter; f, q, w, x and z are not called to use. According to this scheme:

Devanagari	Translit-eration	Sounds Like	Devanagari	Translit-eration	Sounds Like
अ	a	son	ढ्	ḍh	adhesive*
आ	ā	father	ण्	ṇ	under*
इ	i	different	त्	t	tabla
ई	ī	feel	थ्	th	thumb
उ	u	full	द्	d	this
ऊ	ū	boot	ध्	dh	Gandhi
ऋ	ṛ	rhythm*	न्	n	nose
ॠ	ṝ	**	प्	p	pen
ऌ	ḷ	**	फ्	ph	phantom*
ए	e	evade	ब्	b	boil
ऐ	ai	delight	भ्	bh	abhor
ओ	o	core	म्	m	mind
औ	au	now	य्	y	yes
क्	k	calm	र्	r	right
ख्	kh	khan	ल्	l	love
ग्	g	gate	व्	v	very
घ्	gh	ghost	श्	ś	shut
ङ्	ṅ	ankle*	ष	ṣ	sugar
च्	c	chuckle	स्	s	simple
छ्	ch	witch*	ह्	h	happy
ज्	j	justice	ं	ṁ	improvise
झ्	jh	Jhansi	ः	ḥ	**
ञ्	ñ	banyan	क्ष्	kṣ	action
ट्	ṭ	tank	त्र्	tr	three*
ठ्	ṭh	**	ज्ञ्	jñ	gnosis
ड्	ḍ	dog	ऽ	'	a silent 'a'

* These letters don't have an exact English equivalent. An approximation is given here.

** These sounds cannot be approximated in English words.

Introduction

Why would one want to read the *Amṛtabindu Upaniṣad*? We only read books which are well written and well presented, which we can understand, which are interesting and which serve some purpose. A five year old is not likely to read a book on anthropology nor will reading about surgical procedures be meaningful or purposeful for a law student.

What is *Amṛtabindu-upaniṣad*? What does it contain? Is it interesting? Would we understand it? Would its study benefit us? Would it serve any purpose?

The Subject (viṣaya): We expect a book titled 'Modern Physics' to contain knowledge of modern physics. Upaniṣad means Self-knowledge. A book titled Upaniṣad contains Self-knowledge – Knowledge of our true nature.

Even those who claim to know themselves well, only have a vague or partial knowledge of themselves. A doctor may understand his anatomical structure better, a psychologist may claim to know his mind better and an ophthalmologist understands the condition of his eye better. But do we really know the 'I' that knows the body, mind or the eye? The Upaniṣad gives us a clear and complete understanding of who we really are in essence. It goes beyond feelings, ideas, theories and concepts of who we are. It indicates the Self 'as it is' and enables us to directly experience our true nature. It removes all our notions of finitude about ourselves and makes us realise, 'I am the infinite Truth' (brahma-ātma-aikya bodha). Who would not be interested in reading about themselves and discover how great they really are?

The Result (phala): How will the study of the Upaniṣad benefit me? What purpose would it serve? I am what I think I am. I am sad, bad, glad or mad when I think I am so. However, I find that I am happy being happy and cannot stand being unhappy. I cannot bear to live in finitude and sorrow. I want to immediately get rid of sorrow and be happy here and now, and ever after. I actually want infinite and eternal happiness. When I realise that infinite and eternal happiness is my real nature, I am liberated from all notions of finitude and sorrow. To obtain Liberation (mokṣa) is the result of Self-knowledge.

The Seeker (adhikārī): 'If I always do what I always did, I will always get what I always got.' A man complained each day that his lunch box contained the 'same old sandwiches'. His colleague told him, "Why don't you ask your wife to pack something else?" He said, "I am not married. I only pack the sandwiches each day!"

If I seek what I always sought I will get what I always got. Seeking finite goals has always given us finite results which have never given us true satisfaction. Money, name, fame, power, possessions and pleasures have never given us the peace and fulfilment we seek. 'The impermanent can never give us permanent joy.'[1] Then why is my innermost

[1] *na hi adhruvaiḥ prāpyate hi dhruvaṁ tat* – *Kaṭhopaniṣad*-1.2.10

desire for the permanent, the immortal, the infinite? One who questions thus, feels dispassion towards the finite, seeks to know the infinite and so approaches the Guru. Such a person is truly qualified for Self-knowledge. He is most benefitted by this knowledge. The Upaniṣad becomes the nectar that satisfies his inner thirst.

The Upaniṣad: Upaniṣad is Self-knowledge. What does the word Upaniṣad mean? 'Upa' means to go near, to approach a Teacher for Self-knowledge with a heart filled with faith and devotion. 'Ni' means to have firm determination to know the Truth, come what may. 'Ṣad' means to destroy ignorance with the right knowledge. Upaniṣad therefore also indicates the process of gaining Self-knowledge. A book that contains Self-knowledge is also called Upaniṣad.

There are many Upaniṣads in the Vedas. Ten are considered major as they are commented upon by the great Ādi Śaṅkarācārya. Others are called minor even though they contain the same divine Knowledge.

***Amṛtabindu-upaniṣad*:** The five Bindu-upaniṣads found in the *Atharva-veda* are *Nādabindu-upaniṣad, Brahmabindu-upaniṣad, Tejobindu-upaniṣad, Dhyānabindu-upaniṣad* and the *Amṛtabindu-upaniṣad.* They are all minor Upaniṣads and the *Amṛtabindu-upaniṣad* is the most popular amongst them.

Amṛta as a drink is the heavenly nectar or ambrosia. Bindu means a drop. Partaking even a drop of celestial ambrosia makes man immortal, that means it gives him a very long life. The word 'amṛta' means that which is deathless and timeless. It indicates the immortal Truth, realising which one becomes immortal, that is he realises his immortal Self.

Upaniṣads are dialogues between the Teacher and the student (guru-śiṣya saṁvāda) regarding Self-knowledge. The names of the Teacher and student and the story of how they met is not known in this Upaniṣad. Only the immortal Knowledge is reported. Let us also partake of this nectarine Knowledge, even a drop of which can immortalise us.

Invocation Prayer

This beautiful prayer is chanted by both the Guru and the disciples before the class begins. Through this they both tune their minds to the Higher.

ॐ भद्रं कर्णेभिः शृणुयाम देवा भद्रं पश्येमाक्षभिर्यजत्राः ।
स्थिरैरङ्गैस्तुष्टुवाꣳसस्तनूभिर्व्यशेम हि देवहितं यदायुः ॥

स्वस्ति न इन्द्रो वृद्धश्रवाः स्वस्ति नः पूषा विश्ववेदाः ।
स्वस्ति नस्तार्क्ष्यो अरिष्टनेमिः स्वस्ति नो बृहस्पतिर्दधातु ॥

ॐ शान्तिः! शान्तिः!! शान्तिः!!!

oṁ bhadraṁ karṇebhiḥ śṛṇuyāma devā
bhadraṁ paśyemākṣabhir-yajatrāḥ,
sthirairaṅgais-tuṣṭu-vāgm̐sastanūbhir
vyaśema hi devahitaṁ yadāyuḥ.

svasti na indro vṛddhaśravāḥ svasti naḥ pūṣā viśvavedāḥ,
svasti nastārkṣyo ariṣṭanemiḥ svasti no bṛhaspatir-dadhātu.

oṁ śāntiḥ! śāntiḥ!! śāntiḥ!!!

ॐ – symbol of supreme Self; भद्रं – auspicious; कर्णेभिः – with ears; शृणुयाम – may we hear; देवाः – Gods; भद्रम् – auspicious; पश्येम – may we see; अक्षभिः – with eyes; यजत्राः – Oh! Worshipful ones; स्थिरैः – with hale and hearty; अङ्गैः – with the limbs; तुष्टुवां

सः – may we live offering our praises (unto Thee); तनूभिः – by the body; व्यशेम – may we live; देवहितं – for the benefit of God/deities; यदायुः – entire span of life; स्वस्ति – blessings; नः – to us; इन्द्रः – Indra; वृद्धश्रवाः – ancient and famous; स्वस्ति – blessings; नः – to us; पूषा – Sun; विश्ववेदाः – the all-knowing; स्वस्ति – blessings; नः – to us; तार्क्ष्यः – Lord of swift motion (Garuḍa); अरिष्टनेमिः – removes our obstacles; स्वस्ति – blessings; नः – to us; बृहस्पतिः – protector of spiritual wealth (Guru of Gods); दधातु – may (He) give; ॐ – symbol of supreme Self; शान्तिः – peace be; शान्तिः – peace be; शान्तिः – peace be

Oh Gods! By ears may we hear what is auspicious; by eyes may we see what is auspicious; Oh worshipful ones! With the hale and hearty limbs may we live offering our praises (unto Thee). For the benefit of Gods may we have the entire span of life. May the ancient and famous Indra give blessings to us. May the all-knowing Sun give blessings to us. May the Lord of swift motion (Garuḍa), who removes our obstacles give blessings to us. May the protector of spiritual wealth (Guru of Gods) give blessings to us. Let there be Peace, Peace, Peace!

'When we worship or propitiate the Gods, they in turn bless us, empower us and protect us.'[1] Through this prayer we invoke the blessings of the Gods for auspiciousness, strength, health, right attitude, our well-being and peace.

That which is auspicious, purifies our mind and creates peace and love within us. An inauspicious sight creates revulsion and agitation and abusive words create anger. A

[1] *devān-bhāvayatānena te devā bhāvayantu vaḥ* – *Bhagavad-gītā*-3.11

beautiful sunset elevates us and a macabre sight depresses us. *Śrīmad Bhāgavatam* describes how King Pṛthu's entire kingdom was designed and decorated with auspicious symbols so as to create love for God. About fifty years back we found that every Indian home had pictures of Gods and Goddesses in every room. Presently children wake up to rock music, have WWF heroes and pictures of rock stars pasted in their rooms. They dress, speak, think and act like the heroes they idolise. With minds filled with desires, agitations and restlessness, we find them unprepared for the studies that they have to undertake.

We pray that may we be healthy and spend our allotted lifespan in serving Him. King Khaṭvāṅga was powerful and great. He once helped the Gods to win a battle. Pleased with that, they granted him a boon. He asked to know how much of his life was left. They told him that he had but a couple of hours left. He did not ask for an extension. Quite happily he sat to meditate and absorbed his mind in the Lord.

Svasti means well-being. Many a times we really do not know what is good for us. We may desire things which may even harm us. So we pray to the all-knowing and graceful Gods, to become our 'well-wishers' and bless us for our well-being rather than become 'wish-fulfillers' and give us desired things which may harm us.

We pray to Indra, the king of Gods, for strength – free of passion and attachment.[1] We pray to the ever shining Sun God to nourish and empower us with noble intelligence. We

[1] *kāma-rāga vivarjitam* – *Bhagavad-gītā*-7.11

ask of Garuḍa, the divine vehicle of Lord Viṣṇu to quickly remove all obstacles to our material and spiritual progress. We pray to Bṛhaspati, the celestial Guru to bestow on us spiritual knowledge.

Finally we herald peace. May there be no untoward occurances from the phenomenal forces (ādhidaivika), disturbances from the surroundings (ādhibhautika) or difficulties from our body and mind (ādhyātmika). May peace prevail at least whilst we study and reflect on this great knowledge.

Having chanted the peace invocation, the scene is set for the teaching and learning of Self-knowledge. Subtle questions arise only in a calm mind. The disciples ask the Guru, "What is this mind that seems to give us endless troubles? How can we control it? How can we go beyond it?" The Upaniṣad begins with answers to these universally relevant questions –

Verse 1

मनो हि द्विविधं प्रोक्तं शुद्धं चाशुद्धमेव च ।
अशुद्धं कामसङ्कल्पं शुद्धं कामविवर्जितम् ॥ १ ॥

mano hi dvividhaṁ proktaṁ śuddhaṁ cāśuddham-eva ca,
aśuddhaṁ kāmasaṅkalpaṁ śuddhaṁ kāmavivarjitam. (1)

मनः – mind; **हि** – indeed; **द्विविधं** – two types; **प्रोक्तं** – is spoken; **शुद्धं** – pure; **च** – and; **अशुद्धं** – impure; **एव** – only; **कामसङ्कल्पं** – (of the nature of) thoughts of desires; **कामविवर्जितम्** – devoid of desires

1. *Mind indeed is said to be of two types only – (one is) impure with thoughts of desires and (another is) pure, devoid of desires.*

In *Śrīmad Bhāgavatam* there is a beautiful story. Sanak, Sanandan, Sanātana and Sanatkumāra, the four mind born sons of Brahmā – the Creator – once approached him and asked him a similar question, 'How can we separate the mind from all objects and pleasures? They seem to have become one. The mind cannot exist without objects and the objects have no existence without the mind. Objects create desires, agitations, dependency and sorrow in the mind. How can we control this object filled mind?' Interestingly Brahmā whose mind was then preoccupied with the task of creation was unable to answer the question. Brahmā and his sons then prayed to the Lord who appeared before them in the form of a swan (haṁsa) and answered their question. This dialogue is called *Haṁsa-gītā*. He said that when the mind vacillates between mutually dependent things, the solution lies in going beyond both. Instead of the self-defeating exercise of separating the mind from the objects and objects from the mind, we should enquire as to whom do both belong. We come to understand that they are both the conditionings of the individual (jīva). On further enquiry into the essential nature of the individual, we realise that it is the infinite Self within. This enquiry takes us beyond the mind into a realm where all mind created conflicts and confusions cease to exist.

Now here the Guru initiates enquiry with the question, 'What is the mind (manaḥ)?' The word 'manaḥ' comes from the verbal root 'man' – to think. Mind is the faculty in us that thinks thoughts. It is a continuous flow of thoughts. Without thoughts, there is no mind.

As the thought, so the mind. Pure thoughts make it pure and impure thoughts make it impure. What is a pure and impure mind?

A sorrowful mind, with stress, depression, tension, anger, dejection, negative attitudes or with hurtful and harmful thoughts is impure. A mind without these is pure. A pure mind is content, cheerful, peaceful and happy.

An impure mind, like a river in spate is constantly agitated, restless, stormy, distracted, willful and stubborn. A pure mind, free of these is steady, attentive and calm.

A man on his morning walk having strayed too far away from his home gets exhausted. Another keeps his home in sight and returns from his walk, energised and refreshed. Similarly, an impure mind is extrovert and is always running outward, away from its source. A pure mind is introvert and rests in peace in its source.

A mind filled with wrong notions is impure. It entertains thoughts like, 'name, fame, pleasures, comforts, power and position will make me happy!', 'more money means more happiness', 'if I change my house, job or wife, I will become happier', 'when the star position changes, my fate will change', 'my boss is the cause of my failure' and so on. Wrong notions can be removed by right thinking. Right thinking is to realise that 'with money we can buy things, not happiness', 'the state of my mind (mano daśā) cannot solely depend on the position of the stars (graha daśā)', 'if I cannot be happy with myself, how can others be happy in my company?', 'if I cannot make myself happy, who or what else can?', 'if I cannot change myself, no one else can!', 'happiness is not found outside, but within.' Pūjya Gurudev said, "Do not put the key of your happiness in someone else's pocket."

An impure mind is filled with desires (kāma) and fanciful imaginations (saṅkalpa). Saṅkalpas are subtle wishes like, 'why not have this' or 'won't it be good if I get that?' They come to us as gentle suggestions. When brooded upon, they solidify to become desires like, 'I want this' or 'I must have that'. Desires bring in anger, greed, jealousy, cravings and so on. Some desires become compulsive obsessions and addictions. A pure mind is desireless.

Once Sage Maṅki thought, 'Why don't I get a piece of land and grow crops enough to feed me. Then I would not have to go out for alms'. Then he did so. Once as he was tilling the land, a wild camel charged at his bullocks who ran away and they were frightened. The sage ran behind the bullocks to retrieve them. The sage paused in the pursuit of his bullocks with the thought, 'What am I doing? Instead of seeking God, I am running after bullocks! How did I come to this?' He traced the root of his problem to desire and declared, "O desire! I know your source. You verily arise from fanciful ideas. I shall no more entertain them, how then can you trouble me?"[1]

In short, a desire-ridden mind is sorrowful and impure and desireless mind is happy and pure.

[1] *kāma jānāmi te mūlaṁ saṅkalpāt kila jāyase,*
na tvāṁ saṅkalpa iṣyāmi tena me na bhaviṣyasi
– *Mahābhāratam* – *Śānti Parva*-177.25

The next verse is famous and often quoted to show us the very vital role that the mind plays in our life –

Verse 2

मन एव मनुष्याणां कारणं बन्धमोक्षयोः ।
बन्धाय विषयासक्तं मुक्तं निर्विषयं स्मृतम् ॥ २ ॥

mana eva manuṣyāṇāṁ kāraṇaṁ bandhamokṣayoḥ,
bandhāya viṣayāsaktaṁ muktaṁ nirviṣayaṁ smṛtam. (2)

मनः – mind; **एव** – alone; **मनुष्याणां** – of the human beings; **कारणं** – cause; **बन्धमोक्षयोः** – of bondage and Liberation; **बन्धाय** – for bondage; **विषयासक्तं** – attached to sense objects; **मुक्तं** – free; **निर्विषयं** – devoid of desires of objects; **स्मृतम्** – is considered

2. *Mind alone is the cause of bondage and freedom for human beings. Mind attached to sense objects is (the cause of) bondage and devoid of desire for objects is considered free.*

Even though the world appears outside, it is experienced in the mind within. To a man who is unconscious, in deep sleep or in coma, the world does not exist. The day dreamer lives in his day dream, the dreamer in his mind born dream-world, the psychotic in his imagined world and all of us in our subjective world created by our personal likes, dislikes and perceptions. 'As our vision, so the world appears to us.'[1]

[1] *yathā dṛṣṭi tathā sṛṣṭi*

Joys and sorrows, successes and failures, gain and loss, all are experienced within. Even the perception of our body is only in the mind. Therefore Śrī Ramana Maharshi says, "The entire world is only thought modification."[1] Since the world is experienced within, bondage and Liberation too are experienced within.

To the question, 'Do you want mokṣa or Liberation?' most say 'No', as they do not understand what is bondage or Liberation. Bondage is enslavement, restriction, limitation and sorrow, whereas Liberation is freedom from all limitations and sorrow (ātyantika duḥkha nivṛtti) and attainment of unconditional bliss (paramānanda prāpti). Knowing thus, who will not seek Liberation?

What again is bondage and Liberation? Thoughts by themselves cannot bind us or make us happy or unhappy. It is our identification with them as 'me' and 'my' that binds. When a sad thought passes by, we say, 'I am sad' or 'My mind is sad'. It is therefore the identification with the thoughts that causes sorrow. One who knows that he is different from the mind, a witness to the thoughts of the mind, remains unaffected by the mind.

Mind is merely a flow of thoughts albeit at a terrific speed. A single thought by itself is only a fractional flash which has no power to bind us. Only when the thought is repeated, that it becomes strong enough to persecute us. An attentive mind avoids the mindless repetition of negative thoughts and becomes free from their hold.

[1] *manomayam tat bhuvanaṁ samastam – Saddarśanam*-8

Bondage is restriction, enslavement and limitation. A prisoner feels restrained as he is locked in by others with no freedom to go out. Whereas we feel free as we can go out or come into our house without restriction. A child cries out when he is restrained from running helter-skelter by his mother. People rebel against rules that curb their freedom. A person with a fixed salary is strained by rising inflation whereas one who has access to an unlimited expense account spends freely. Some are bound physically, others are duty bound, time bound or family bound, yet others are economically dependent or politically enslaved or are socially outcasts. But the biggest bondage that we all experience is the slavery of the mind. We are limited by our imagination, restricted by our pettiness, attached to our opinions, enslaved by our whims and fancies, bound by our emotions, whipped up by our passions, bogged down by our insecurities, harassed by our fears and tortured by our sorrows.

How does the mind get bound to objects? Lack of thinking, incomplete thinking or wrong thinking leads to bondage. Right and complete thinking liberates.[1] What is wrong thinking? We give a separate existence to the objects of the world, that is, we consider that they exist outside us (sattā adhyāsa). Thereafter we superimpose our personal likes and dislikes on them (śobhana/aśobhana adhyāsa). We further superimpose joy and sorrow on them (sukha/duḥkha adhyāsa). Thereafter we cannot help but desire them as to seek happiness which is inherent in all of us. Desires (kāma) lead to actions (karma) which give results (phala) which when enjoyed or suffered leave impressions (vāsanās)

[1] *avicārakṛto bandhaḥ vicāreṇa nivartate – Pañcadaśī*-10.5

which give rise to more desires, actions, impressions and so on. This repeated thinking and enjoying creates attachment. For example, I see a TV in the neighbour's house, like it, think that it would be good to have the same model in my home, desire it, earn to buy it, then buy it, enjoy it and get slowly attached to it.

Attachment to objects makes us dependent on them, causes fear of loosing them, jealous of others who have more of them and unhappy, empty and lost when we lose them. It gives rise to obsessive thinking, compulsive desires and helpless actions. 'Even though the rational intellect rejects, man is forced into sin prompted by compulsive desires.'[1] The object (viṣaya) may be a physical thing, a pleasure, a person, an emotion, an ideology, a concept or an opinion. People are seen to become fanatic and resort to terrorist activities when attached to some political or religious ideology.

Aṣṭāvakra Mahārāja advises King Janaka, "O son! If you aspire for Liberation, reject sense objects just as you would reject poison."[2] In fact the sense objects are more dangerous than poison. Poison kills only when partaken whereas the sense objects bind us even when we see, smell, taste, hear, touch or think about them.

How can we free ourselves from the sense objects and our strong attachments to them? Renouncing the object is the first step to getting rid of the attachment to the object.[3]

1 *anicchannapi vārṣṇeya balāt iva [kāmaḥ] niyojitaḥ* – *Bhagavad-gītā*-3.36

2 *muktim icchasi cet tāta viṣayān viṣavat tyajet* – *Aṣṭāvakra-gītā*-2

3 *tattu viṣaya-tyāgāt saṅga-tyāgāt ca* – *Nārada-bhakti-sūtra*-35

For example, not smoking is the first step to kicking the smoking habit. Right thinking, patience, determination and an attentive mind will then help us get rid of the attachment.

Is joy or sorrow in objects? Did I not live happily even before I bought the TV or mobile? I call myself a free person, then how can I remain enslaved by the whims and fancies of my mind? All bondage, sorrow and tensions are mind created. How can I blame anyone for my self-inflicted sorrows? What is self made, can also be redone or undone. Positive thoughts, sāttvika lifestyle, conducive inputs and constant vigilance will break wrong, negative and compulsive thought patterns.

A mind free of attachments is happy and peaceful.[1] A saint was walking. Suddenly he turned around and started walking back. When asked if he had forgotten something or lost his way, he said, "The direction of wind changed and my hair was coming into my eyes, so I changed direction. I have nowhere to go, so I am never lost!"

---

[1] *tyāgāt śāntiranantaram – Bhagavad-gītā*-12.12

Can we become free from the bondages of our mind once and for all? How can we do so?

Verse 3

यतो निर्विषयस्यास्य मनसो मुक्तिरिष्यते ।
अतो निर्विषयं नित्यं मनः कार्यं मुमुक्षुणा ॥ ३ ॥

yato nirviṣayasyāsya manaso muktiriṣyate,
ato nirviṣayaṁ nityaṁ manaḥ kāryaṁ mumukṣuṇā. (3)

यतः – since; अस्य निर्विषयस्य – of the one free from sense objects; मनसः – mind; मुक्तिः – freedom; इष्यते – goes to; अतः – therefore; निर्विषयं – free from (desires of) sense objects; नित्यं – all the time; मनः – mind; कार्यं – should be practised; मुमुक्षुणा – by the seeker of Liberation

3. *Mind, free from desire of sense objects becomes free. Therefore, a seeker of Liberation should constantly practise to make his mind free from sense objects.*

A mistake can always be corrected. A problem can be solved or resolved. A wrong can be righted. The impure mind too can be purified.

Water by its very nature is pure, refreshing, nourishing and life-giving. It adds taste to all that we eat. When chemicals, dirt or bacteria come in contact with it, it gets polluted and can cause diseases. However, the pollutants only remain suspended in water, and do not bring any intrinsic change to it. The pollutants can be removed by household methods like boiling, straining and use of alum or desalination and distillation plants. If water was impure by its very nature, or if the pollutants had changed the very structure of water, it would be impossible to purify it.

Similarly, the mind by its very nature is pure. Desires, attachments and the like pollute it. They however cannot change its inherent pure nature. If the mind was impure by its very nature or if desires or attachments would remain permanently in the mind, then it would not be possible to remove them and we would have had to accept its sorrowful and stressed condition as natural. Luckily, desires, attachments, sorrow and stress can be removed and the mind can be purified.

How should we purify the mind? We should first become aware of its impure state and feel bad about it. If we do not accept the impurity for what it is, and justify it or consider it normal, then we will do nothing about it. Once we realise that we need to rid ourselves of desires and attachments, we should put forth the right efforts to remove them. Either consciously or unconsciously the mind has picked up many impurities. They will not go on their own. Conscious, consistent, determined and patient efforts will have to be put forth to purify the mind.

Most of us only desire temporary and immediate relief from tension and sorrow, so we adopt quick fix methods like drinks, pleasures and the like. Such methods only seem to increase desires and tensions. A person who wants to get rid of sorrow once and for all, goes to the root of the problem and adopts methods with more permanent results. Such a seeker of Liberation is called a mumukṣu and the various methods he adopts to purify the mind are called sādhanās.

The preliminary sādhanās that can be practised by beginners are worship (pūjā), repetition of a mantra (japa), remembrance of God's name (nāma smaraṇa), visiting holy places (tīrtha yātrā), singing the glories of God (kīrtana), ritualistic sacrifices (yajña), charity (dāna), austerities (tapas) and so on. One or a combination of these practices can be used to purify the mind.

A mind relatively purified by the preliminary spiritual practices is ready for the subtler practice of meditation which the Guru expounds in the next two verses –

Verse 4 & 5

निरस्त विषयासङ्गं सन्निरुद्धं मनो हृदि ।
यदाऽयात्यात्मनो भावं तदा तत्परमं पदम् ॥ ४ ॥

तावदेव निरोद्धव्यं यावत् हृदि गतं क्षयम् ।
तज्ज्ञानं च ध्यानं च शेषो न्यायश्च विस्तरः ॥ ५ ॥

nirasta viṣayāsaṅgaṁ sanniruddhaṁ mano hṛdi,
yadā'yātyātmano bhāvaṁ tadā tatparamaṁ padam. (4)

tāvad-eva niroddhavyaṁ yāvat hṛdi gataṁ kṣayam,
etajjñānaṁ ca dhyānaṁ ca śeṣo nyāyaśca vistaraḥ. (5)

निरस्त – having renounced; विषयासङ्गं – attachment to sense objects; सन्निरुद्धं – well controlled; मनः – mind; हृदि – in the heart; यदा – when; आयाति – (he) obtains; आत्मनः – of the Self; भावं – nature; तदा – then; तत् – (he attains) that; परमं पदम् – supreme abode तावत् – so long; एव – only; निरोद्धव्यं – should be restrained; यावत् – thus long; हृदि – in the heart; गतं क्षयम् – gets dissolved; एतत् – this; ज्ञानं – knowledge; च – and; ध्यानं – meditation; च – and; शेषः – the rest; न्यायः – logic; च – and; विस्तरः– elaboration

4. *Having renounced attachment to sense objects, when the mind is well controlled in the heart, it obtains the nature of the Self – the supreme abode.*

5. *The mind should be restrained only as long as it gets dissolved in the heart. This is knowledge and meditation; the rest is (mere) logic and (verbal) elaboration.*

Mind and Meditation

Meditation is to withdraw the mind from objects and turn it towards the subject, the Self within. An idle mind is a devil's workshop. A mind free from objects and attachments to objects needs to be occupied and a place to rest. Without that it would run away into its usual fields of preoccupations and habits, wandering about restlessly in the world of objects. Home is where the heart is. When the mind reaches its home, the Self within, it rests peacefully.

For example, a child plays joyfully with his toys and friends, totally forgetful of his homework and home. Being engrossed in play, he ignores his mother's frequent calls to return home.[1] Forgetting his hunger or tiredness, the child plays with his toys. However, when it becomes dark, and hunger and tiredness catches on, even when his friends beckon him, he leaves them and returns home. There he is embraced by his mother's love and care and he rests peacefully.

Mind and Heart

Mind is a flow of thoughts. Thoughts are of objects. However, the locus of this flow of thoughts of objects is the heart or the Self within. How do we locate this locus? There where we experience the thought 'I am' 'I am' is the heart, the very centre of our being and existence.

[1] *kṣudhāṁ dehavyathāṁ tyaktvā bālaḥ krīḍati vastuni – Vivekacūḍāmaṇi*-538

Physically we indicate the mind to be located in the head. Ask a person to remember something. He will scratch his head. When he thinks a lot, he gets a headache. Mental calculations happen in the head. However, where do we experience 'I', the Self? When called by name, universally we put our hand on the heart and say, 'I am here'.

Physically the head and the heart may have a separate location, but the locus of the mind with all its thoughts is centred in the Self, the spiritual heart within, the place where we experience the 'I' in its purest form, free from all thoughts. It is in the presence of 'I' that we think thoughts. Without 'I' there are no thoughts. Objects that the mind thinks about are different but the 'I' that knows them and gives existence to them is the same.

Mind and its Nature

What is the true nature of the mind – restlessness or peace? Most of us would think that it is restless and listless, changing and desiring, agitated and distracted by its very nature. However, the fact that each one of us has experienced peace and quietude, although fleeting, proves that peace (not agitation), is its true nature. To attain its true nature (ātmano bhāvam) is the supreme goal, the final destination of man (paramaṁ padam).

Mind is a flow of thoughts. Thought = subject + object. The mind becomes impure, restless or attached only when it comes in contact with objects. Free of all objects, the mind is no mind. It becomes of the nature of the subject, the pure Self. The Self is of the nature of Existence-Consciousness-

Bliss. Hence the true nature of the mind too is Existence-Consciousness-Bliss. The practice of identifying with one's true nature is called meditation and its culmination in the effortless awareness of one's true nature is also called meditation. Hence meditation is the final means, the highest spiritual practice and also the ultimate goal of all spiritual pursuits.

Knowledge and Meditation

To renounce what you are not and to be what you really are – the infinite Truth – is called Self-realisation or meditation. Many consider Self-knowledge and meditation to be different. But the Upaniṣad asserts that they are the same (etat jñānaṁ ca dhyānaṁ ca).

Devotion is to become one with the infinite supreme Truth, that is, to realise that I am of the nature of infinite Truth, which is Self-realisation. Therefore, Tulasīdāsa says that there is no difference between knowledge and devotion.[1]

For how long should I meditate? Meditation as a spiritual practice is to be done till we realise the supreme Truth as our own Self. Meditation or knowledge as a state of Realisation thereafter is never lost.

Once the true nature of the mind is realised, the mind and its agitations can no longer bind us. It is the Self alone that has taken the form of the various thoughts of the mind. For example, one who realises that water is the essence in

[1] *jñānihi bhaktihi nahi kachu bhedā* – Saint Tulasīdāsa

all waves of the ocean, sees water alone in and through all the waves. He knows that waves are nothing but different forms assumed by the water.

Logic and Discussion

Logic and discussion are tools used to arrive at the truth of a topic. Their purpose is served once the Truth is determined. Thereafter they are redundant and can be discarded. The Truth when determined intellectually must be realised as one's own Self through meditation or knowledge. One who remains engrossed forever in scholastic discussions and debates never realises the Truth.

The wise man having realised the Truth never gets into fruitless discussions or arguments.[1] What he has realised is beyond the purview of the mind and intellect, indeed it is beyond the scope of logic and discussion.

A scholar came to Saint Kabīradāsa to engage him in scriptural debate. Kabīradāsa told him, "Your goal is to win. I accept defeat. Why start the discussion?"

Discussions which help us gain clarity are fine. Others which create conflict and confusions or increase our pride and prejudices are in vain.

---

[1] *vijānan vidvān bhavate nātivādī – Muṇḍakopaniṣad*-3.1.4

How should I meditate? On what should I meditate? How can I realise my own true nature? The Guru says –

Verse 6

नैव चिन्त्यं न चाचिन्त्यं न चिन्त्यं चिन्त्यमेव तत्।
पक्षपातविनिर्मुक्तं ब्रह्म संपद्यते तदा ॥ ६ ॥

naiva cintyaṁ na cācintyaṁ na cintyaṁ cintyam-eva tat,
pakṣapāta-vinirmuktaṁ brahma sampadyate tadā. (6)

न – not; एव – indeed; चिन्त्यं – to be thought of (with likes); न – not; च – and; अचिन्त्यं – not to be thought of (due to dislikes); न – not; चिन्त्यं – to be thought of (as object); चिन्त्यं एव – should be contemplated; तत् – That; पक्षपातविनिर्मुक्तं – devoid of any partiality; ब्रह्म – Brahman, the Self; संपद्यते – attains; तदा – then

6. *Neither to be thought of (with likes) nor to be not thought of (due to dislikes), not to be thought of (as object) and should be contemplated (as the subject, Reality). Then one attains Brahman, the Self which is devoid of any partiality.*

The Self-realisation with or without the mind?

Ignorance of the Self expresses in the mind as thoughts like, 'I am finite', 'I am the body' or 'I am born'. Contemplation on the Self as 'I am the infinite Self' removes the thought 'I am finite.' This shows that even though the Self is beyond the mind,[1] yet it can be realised only through the mind.[2] It cannot be thought of (na cintyam), yet should be thought of (cintyam eva tat).

The Self – the object or the subject?

In meditation the mind contemplates on the Self within. Does that make the mind the object or the subject of meditation?

The mind only knows how to objectify. It knows all – the gross world of objects with names, forms and qualities and the subtle world of concepts and emotions – as objects. Therefore the mind attempts to know the knower – Self, the subject also as an object. The Upaniṣad declares that the subject not being a gross or a subtle object cannot ever be known or thought of as an object (na cintyam). The light from the torchlight cannot illumine the battery cells within the torch.

The dormant and unmanifest impressions (vāsanās) are beyond the purview of the mind (acintya). When the unmanifest impressions themselves cannot be known by the mind, how can the Self, their locus become an object of the mind?

Because the Self cannot be contemplated upon as an object (na cintyam), it does not mean that It cannot be thought of. It should be thought of as the very subject that illumines all objects (cintyam eva tat).

---

[1] *yanmanasā na manute – Kenopaniṣad*-1.5

[2] *manasā eva āptavyam – Kaṭhopaniṣad*-2.1.11

The Self – unknown, well-known or less known?

'I know Sanskrit well, I more or less understand English but I do not know a word of Chinese.' Objects of the world can be known in degrees as more or less or can become an object of our ignorance. The Self can only be known 'as it is', so it cannot be known in degrees as 'I know It a little' or 'I know It well'. One has either realised the Self or not realised It at all. However, strangely none can say that they do not know the Self. Do I not know that 'I am' and 'I know that I am'?

The Self – different or one?

The knower is always different from the known. For example, the book that I see is different from me. The objects of the world which include my body and my thoughts, are known, and therefore, different from me, the knower. The knower Self, therefore, cannot become the known (na cintyam). I cannot sit on my own back. That does not mean that the mind cannot think of the Self (na acintyam). The Self is to be thought of as, 'I am the infinite Self', not as 'I know the infinite Self' (cintyam eva tat).

The Self – the means or the source of happiness?

We like what gives us joy, dislike what makes us unhappy and we are indifferent to what gives neither. For example, 'I like to eat mangoes, dislike even the thought of eating a fish and am indifferent towards salads.' 'I like being in love, dislike feeling humiliated and am indifferent towards mathematical concepts'. We can even like and dislike our body and the thoughts of our mind. The Self is not a means of joy (sukha sādhana) like mangoes, and therefore, does not become an object of like, dislike or indifference. The Self is of the very nature of happiness (sukha svarūpa), and therefore, the very source of all joy (sukha mūla).

What we like at one time we can dislike some other time. Our likes and dislikes keep changing as our concepts of what gives joy and sorrow changes. However, the love that we have for the Self never changes. It is unconditional and total as it does not depend on time, place and circumstances. I love myself irrespective of anything because it is the very source of happiness. Hence the Self should be contemplated upon as, 'I am absolute Bliss' (cintyam eva tat).

The Self – the contradictory or uncontradicted?

The Truth or the Self cannot be conceptualised, yet the mind tries to form some concept of the Self. The Guru therefore breaks this habit of the mind through apparently contradictory statements.

The Self is said to be unthinkable (na cintyam) and yet not unthinkable (na acintyam), cannot be thought of, yet to be thought of (cintyam eva tat). Samartha Rāmadāsa says, "Without becoming a thinker, think of That which cannot be thought of." Contemplation on such subtle and apparently contradictory statements takes us to a mindless state wherein we realise the Truth or the Self which stands uncontradicted by any concepts or ideas (pakṣapāta-vinirmuktaṁ brahma).

The mind thinks in terms of opposites and comparisons. When it is said that a person is not tall, we form an image of a short man. So when it is said that a person is neither tall nor short nor of medium height, we do not know what to think. A person is called tall only with reference to a short man. When the point of reference is removed, we are unable to conceptualise. A mind free of concepts realises the Self.

The Self – opposed or unopposed?

The very existence of another creates duality and duals. For example, the birth of the second child creates sibling rivalry. What is different from another, contradicts, opposes and stands apart. For example, people in a different political party stand apart and oppose. The Self is not a 'different thing', but the Self of all and one with all. It is that which gives existence to all, it is unopposed to anything, it does not negate or contradict anything. For example, fuel ignites fire, air blows it and water douses it. Earth, water, air and fire are different from each other. But they all exist in space which accomodates all; opposes, resists, or restricts none. Someone asked the great Saint Udiya Baba, "Do you believe in dualism or non-dualism?" He said, "I do not believe in any 'ism'. I am the non-dual Truth beyond all 'isms'."

Truth or the Self is impartial to all. It gives existence to all and illumines all – the good, bad or the ugly. The Lord declares in the *Gītā*, "I am impartial to all. I do not dislike or like anyone."[1] We should meditate on the Self as, 'I am the non-dual Self opposed to none and impartial to all' (pakṣapāta-vinirmuktaṁ).

[1] *na me dveṣyosti na priyaḥ – Bhagavad-gītā*-9.29

Meditation on the Self as, 'I am the infinite Truth or the Self' is the subtlest and direct means to Self-realisation. To one who is unable to practise this, a simpler, yet powerful meditation technique is recommended –

Verse 7

स्वरेण सन्धयेत् योगम् अस्वरं भावयेत्परम् ।
अस्वरेणानुभावेन भावो वाऽभाव इष्यते ॥ ७ ॥

svareṇa sandhayet yogam asvaraṁ bhāvayetparam,
asvareṇānubhāvena bhāvo vā'bhāva iṣyate. (7)

स्वरेण – by the sound; योगम् सन्धयेत् – the union must be established; अस्वरं – one beyond the sound; भावयेत् – should be meditated; परम् – Supreme; अस्वरेणानुभावेन – by meditating on That which is beyond sound; भावः – existence; वा – and; अभावः – non-existence; इष्यते – becomes

7. *Initially the union with the Higher should be established by concentrating on the sound (of Om). Then, one should meditate upon that Supreme that is beyond sound. By meditating on That which is beyond sound, the non-existence (illusory appearance of world) becomes existence (as the reality).*

Yoga

Union with the Higher is called 'yoga' and with the grosser 'bhoga.' Here absorption of the mind in the Truth or the Self is called yoga. Even the practice of absorbing the mind is called yoga. The best of minds can attain yoga effortlessly. However, the majority of us need a support (ālambana) as the direct and immediate means is difficult. For example, the bird with strong wings effortlessly flies to the treetop whereas the baby bird flies from branch to branch, gradually. The ant too reaches the same height at its own pace in its own way.

Svara

The Guru recommends the support of sound (svara) to reach the Truth or the Self. The word 'svara' has many meanings. In Indian classical music, the musical notes are called svaras. The mantras of the Vedas are set to metrical scales called svaras. The vowels of the Sanskrit language are also called svaras.

Om

Here svara means the universal sound symbol 'Om' which represents the supreme Truth or the Self.[1] Om is the name of God or the Truth.[2] Om is the essence of the Vedas and the glory of the Lord.[3] Om represents the ultimate goal.[4] Therefore, Om is both the means and the goal. Om as a letter is a visual support and Om as a sound is an audio support in meditation. It is said that the Creator chanted Om before starting His creation.

---

[1] *om iti brahma* – *Taittirīya-upaniṣad*-1.16

[2] *tasya vācakaḥ praṇavaḥ* – *Patañjali-yoga-sūtra*-1.27

[3] *praṇavaḥ sarvavedeṣu* – *Bhagavad-gītā*-7.8

[4] *sarve vedā yat-padam-āmananti tapāṁsi sarvāṇi ca yad-vadanti,*
yad-icchanto brahmacaryaṁ caranti tatte padaṁ saṅgraheṇa bravīmi-om-ityetat
– *Kaṭhopaniṣad*-1.2.15

The sounds (mātrās) 'a', 'u' and 'm' put together produces the holy sound Om (a + u = o + m = Om). Om is chanted in a long resonating sound like a temple bell or a conch. The silence between the chanting of two Oms is called amātrā. The mātrās 'a', 'u' and 'm' represent the gross, subtle and the unmanifest world and the waking, dream and deep sleep states respectively. Amātrā is the Truth or the Self beyond the gross, subtle or unmanifest potential and the three states. It underlies and pervades creation and the three states. It is the Truth or the Self from which creation emerges, in which it exists and into which it merges.

Meditation

When the mind is rested and refreshed, choose a solitary place and a quiet time to meditate. Early morning in natural surroundings is good as nature too aids our efforts. Sit in a comfortable seat and posture with the back straight. Relax the body and remain still. Resolve that you will not move your body. Watch the rhythmic movement of your breath. Pray to God and your Guru for blessings and guidance. Just as you give 'quality time' to your family, make meditation an 'exclusive time' for God, Truth or the Self. Bring to your mind thoughts like, 'I do not belong to anyone and no one belongs to me at this time. I am neither a man or woman, a parent or son. I am right now only a seeker of Truth or the Self. What I do is most important and nothing else is more important presently.' These thoughts will help the mind to remain focussed.

Om Meditation

Make the mind relatively pure, subtle and concentrated through the above mentioned or any other preparatory steps. Start chanting Om loudly and slowly. Focus the mind exclusively on the sound. Listen with attention and concentration. That itself will calm the mind further. Thereafter shift the focus of your attention to the silence between the chanting of two Oms. Become intensely aware of this silence. The chanting gradually becomes slower, the duration of the silence increases and finally the chanting stops and silence alone remains. The mind thereafter abides in that silence. When this practice is done without understanding of the deeper import of Om, it leads to jaḍa samādhi – a state of absorption without Realisation. When meditation is practised with knowledge, it leads to Realisation as, 'I am the infinite silence from which all names, forms, sounds and states of experience emerge. I am the peace that passeth all understanding.'

Realisation

Meditation on silence leads to Realisation. What is Realisation? The initiate on the path considers the world alone as real. For him the Truth or the Self is non-existent or unreal. As he enquires, he understands the changing nature of the world and accepts the existence of a changeless Truth or the Self that underlies the world. When he starts meditating, the thoughts and world appear more illusory and the Truth or the Self becomes more real. As his meditation deepens, the world appears unreal and the Truth or the Self becomes self-evident. On realisation of the Truth or the Self, the world ceases to exist. The division of the Real and unreal disappears. The Truth or the Self alone remains (bhāvo vā'bhāva iṣyate). The world, if experienced is also recognised as the Truth alone.[1]

Svara Sādhanā

Musicians meditate on musical notes as the Truth (Self) (nāda-brahma-upāsanā). The music created through the notes (āhata svara) is mastered through deep understanding and devoted practice. This in time leads them to the silence underlying all notes. Meditating on this silence or uncreated sound (anāhata nāda) leads them to Realisation as 'I am this infinite silence from which all music emerge.' Śrī Gurudev called music 'the ornamentation of silence.'

[1] *brahmaivāham idaṁ jagacca sakalaṁ cinmātra vistāritam – Manīṣā-pañcakam*-2

What is the nature of this infinite silence or Truth? What is that Reality which is realised when the world disappears? The Guru says –

Verse 8

तदेव निष्कलं ब्रह्म निर्विकल्पं निरञ्जनम् ।
तत् ब्रह्माहमिति ज्ञात्वा ब्रह्म संपद्यते ध्रुवम् ॥ ८ ॥

tadeva niṣkalaṁ brahma nirvikalpaṁ nirañjanam,
tat brahmāhamiti jñātvā brahma sampadyate dhruvam. (8)

तत् – That; एव – alone; निष्कलं – partless; ब्रह्म – Brahman; निर्विकल्पं – free of differences; निरञ्जनम् – taintless; तत् – That; ब्रह्म – Brahman; अहम् – I am; इति – thus; ज्ञात्वा – knowing; ब्रह्म – Brahman; संपद्यते – (one) attains; ध्रुवम् – Eternal

8. *That alone is Brahman which is free of differences, without parts and taintless. On knowing 'I am that Brahman', one attains the Eternal.*

Reality

Truth or Reality is that which is infinite.[1] Truth is that which supports the entire world as its substratum.[2]

Knowing Reality

Truth is subtler than the subtlest. Subtle ways are used to indicate the Truth. One such way is the method of negation

[1] *bṛhatvāt brahma*

[2] *bharaṇatvāt brahma*

(neti neti). All that is not the Truth is negated and what remains thereafter is realised as the Truth.

The individual or total gross body is made up of various limbs and parts. The Truth is partless (niṣkala), hence neither gross body nor the gross world. The individual and total subtle body is made up of thoughts. The Truth is without thoughts (nirvikalpa), therefore, it is neither the individual subtle body nor the total subtle world. The individual and total causal bodies are the unmanifest impressions (vāsanās) which are the causes of the gross and subtle bodies and the world respectively. It is of the nature of ignorance of the Truth, which itself is the impurity which causes man to sin. The Truth is pure (nirañjana), hence not the causal body. When the gross, subtle and causal bodies are thus negated, the Truth is realised as the substratum of all the three.

Knowing Reality as Me

When I know that Śrī Patel is rich, my poverty is not removed. When I know that he is my long lost father, I become a billionaire. Intellectual knowledge (parokṣa jñāna) that the infinite Truth is the substratum of the three bodies alone does not free me from their bondage. To realise that I am the infinite Truth liberates me from all limitations. Direct knowledge (aparokṣa jñāna) alone liberates us once and for all times to come (dhruvam).

This knowledge is indeed astounding. We feel good when we think we are great. Imagine the experience of the Master who knows he is the greatest – the infinite Truth! We feel good and complimented when others tell us we are good or great. Similarly, even listening to Self-knowledge makes us feel good. Even its intellectual knowledge helps us face life positively. For example, I know of a person who went through a tough operation keeping in mind the thought, 'I am not the body.' We thank people who compliment us about ourselves or our possessions. Imagine the feeling of gratefulness that the Realised one feels towards his Guru who liberates him with the Knowledge, 'You are the infinite Truth, the true Self!'

Can the Truth be proved logically? If not, is not the Truth illogical? The Guru says –

Verse 9

निर्विकल्पमनन्तं च हेतुदृष्टान्तवर्जितम् ।
अप्रमेयमनादिं च यज्ज्ञात्वा मुच्यते बुधः ॥ ९ ॥

nirvikalpam-anantaṁ ca hetudṛṣṭāntavarjitam,
aprameyam-anādiṁ ca yajjñātvā mucyate budhaḥ. (9)

निर्विकल्पम् – devoid of division; अनन्तं – endless; च – and; हेतुदृष्टान्तवर्जितम् – beyond logic and comparison; अप्रमेयम् – immeasurable (or unparalleled); अनादिं – without beginning; च – and; यत् – that which; ज्ञात्वा – having known; मुच्यते – is liberated; बुधः – a wise one

9. *Devoid of division, without beginning, endless, immeasurable, beyond logic and comparison is Brahman – knowing which a wise one is liberated.*

Truth is infinite (anantam)

The finite is limited by time, space and objects. What is born shall perish. The book that is printed will go out of print. What appears, also disappears in time. When love ends, the couple divorce. New theories replace old ones. Everything in the world is conditioned by time.

When I am in Mumbai, I am not in Delhi. A person does not extend beyond his nose! Every object, however big, is limited space wise.

The very existence of an object limits the other object. The ruler or the ruling party's sovereignty is limited by the existence of another leader or an opposition party, however weak and small.

The Truth is timeless and eternal, formless and all-pervading, objectless and non-dual. It is therefore infinite and unconditioned by time, space or objects.

Truth is beyond logic (hetu-varjitam)

Each area of knowledge is known in a different way. Skills are acquired by practice, the beauty of poetry is appreciated through feelings, the laws of science are proved through the method of observation, experimentation, logic and analysis, God is known through faith and the Truth is realised through direct experience. We cannot appreciate a painting through logic or prove historical facts by perception or experimentation. This does not mean that art and history are illogical and unscientific. They are beyond the scope of logic and experimentation.

Many worldly knowledges are beyond the purview of logic, then what to talk of the infinite Truth or the Self which is beyond the scope of the senses, mind and intellect. It is surely beyond logic, yet not illogical.

Truth is incomparable (dṛṣṭānta-varjitam)

Comparison is always between two objects. The Truth is non-dual, one without a second, and therefore, incomparable. We compare the qualities of two objects. For example, he is brave like a lion or stinks like a skunk. The Truth is objectless and attributeless, and therefore, incomparable.

Truth is beyond logic and example (hetu-dṛṣṭānta-varjitam)

A person said that there was fire on the mountain without even seeing the fire. He proved his statement (pratijñā) with logic (hetu) and example (dṛṣṭānta). His logic is that the fact that he sees smoke, shows that there must be fire as without fire there cannot be smoke. He further proves it by citing an example saying wherever there is fire there is always smoke like in a lighted cigarette. Inferred knowledge is based on perception and logic. The infinite Truth or the Self cannot be proved by such logic or example, since it is beyond perception of the senses and inference of the mind. Being non-dual and one of its kind, it is not comparable to anything else.

Truth is immeasurable and unknown (aprameyam)

Instruments or the mind can measure an object which is finite and has measurable qualities. For example, the man is 6 feet tall and weighs 100 pounds. The Truth is not an object. It is infinite and attributeless, and therefore, immeasurable. 'I', the knower, knows the outside objects, the condition of my senses and the thoughts of my mind. How can the objects and the mind which are known, know the knower Self which illumines them? It is therefore unknown (verse 6).

Truth is beginningless (anādi)

Birth is the coming into being of a thing which did not exist before. For example, yesterday the dog gave birth to a litter of puppies. The Truth is eternal and ever exists and is therefore unborn and beginningless.

The knower of Truth (budhaḥ)

Can the infinite ever be bound? The Realised Master who knows 'I am infinite', realises that he was always liberated.

The following mantra is very powerful and ascertains the nature of the Truth in no uncertain terms. It is also quoted by Gauḍapādācārya in his famous Kārikā (commentary) on the *Māṇḍūkya-upaniṣad*.

Verse 10

न निरोधो न चोत्पत्तिः न बद्धो न च साधकः ।
न मुमुक्षुर्न वै मुक्तः इत्येषा परमार्थता ॥ १० ॥

na nirodho na cotpattiḥ na baddho na ca sādhakaḥ,
na mumukṣurna vai muktaḥ ityeṣā paramārthatā. (10)

न – not; निरोधः – dissolution; न – not; च – and; उत्पत्तिः – creation; न – not; बद्धः – bound; न – not; च – and; साधकः – spiritual practitioner; न – not; मुमुक्षुः – seeker of Liberation; न – not; वै – verily; मुक्तः – liberated; इति – thus; एषा – this is; परमार्थता – supreme Truth

10. *This state of supreme Truth is one where there is no dissolution nor creation, no one bound, nor a spiritual practitioner, none a seeker of Liberation nor indeed a liberated one!*

In my dream, I was appearing for an exam. I entered the examination hall. There were many other students and a supervisor. First the answer sheets were distributed. That was not a problem as I only had to write my examination number. The real problem started when the question paper was distributed. I had prepared for physics and the paper was for chemistry. The entire chemistry of my body changed and I fainted. The supervisor splashed water on my face and I woke up from my dream! On waking, I saw that there was no exam or examination hall, no students or supervisor, no question paper or answer sheets – I alone existed. My self-created dream did not really exist, even though it seemed so real and frightening. Similarly from the standpoint of the absolute Truth, there is no creation or dissolution, none who is bound nor liberated, nor is there any seeker or sought.

There is no creation or dissolution (na nirodho na cotpattiḥ)

This seems inconceivable and very difficult to digest for most of us for whom the world is solid and totally real. How can the world which seems so real, have no existence at all? How can I believe something which is against every experience of mine? The same scriptures that say that the world does not exist, give theories of creation and dissolution and action and reaction. They speak of right conduct, good deeds, concepts of right and wrong and how to cultivate values and virtues and live happily in this world. They also call the world changing and relatively real.

The above are only explanations for our experience of the world. When the Truth is realised, even the relative reality of the world is negated. We know that from the standpoint of the Truth, creation never did exist. This is the absolute Truth. For example, a man sees a snake where there is only a rope. The snake exists only in the vision of the seer. Many explanations can be given for his vision but when he sees the rope, the snake vision disappears. From the standpoint of the rope, the snake never did exist.

Svāmī Akhandananda could speak with knowledge and depth on various Indian philosophies and scriptures. He was asked, "You speak of different philosophies with ease and conviction. You even talk of ajāta-vāda, the belief that creation never existed. What is your true belief?" He said, "The Truth is not a belief (vāda) or a school of thought (mata). I do not believe in ajāta-vāda, I am ajāta – unborn!"

That which is born must perish. The Truth is beginningless and eternal (verse 9), uncreated and indestructible, unborn and immortal.

There is no seeker (sādhaka) nor the sought (sādhya)

We can attain only that which is away from us in time and place. Means are adopted only when you have a goal to reach. We take the help of ropes to climb and reach the mountain top. We have to contest in an election and win in order to become Member of the Parliament. We have to study the course material and give exams to get a degree. But how can I become a seeker if there is nothing to seek? How can I attain something which is already gained? The Truth is one with me and ever attained by me (nitya prāpta). Therefore from the standpoint of the Truth, there is no seeker, seeking or sought.

None is bound nor seeker of Liberation nor liberated (na baddhaḥ na mumukṣuḥ na muktaḥ)

The father pretended to tie his two children in fun. The younger one believed he was bound and started crying and asked his father to untie him. The elder one knew well that he was never bound. Only one who thinks he is bound seeks Liberation. One who knows that he is infinite and ever liberated is free from all notions of bondage and Liberation. Only one who feels unhappy seeks to become happy. One who is of the nature of happiness, seeks neither the removal of sorrow nor the gain of happiness. From the standpoint of the infinite Truth, there is none bound or liberated.

The following verse uses the method of 'anvaya-vyatireka' (presence-absence) to arrive at the Truth –

Verse 11

एक एवात्मा मन्तव्यो जाग्रत्स्वप्नसुषुप्तिषु ।
स्थानत्रयव्यतीतस्य पुनर्जन्म न विद्यते ॥ ११ ॥

eka evātmā mantavyo jāgrat-svapna-suṣuptiṣu,
sthānatraya-vyatītasya punarjanma na vidyate. (11)

एक – One; एव – alone; आत्मा – Self; मन्तव्यः – should be known; जाग्रत्स्वप्नसुषुप्तिषु – in waking, dream and deep sleep states; स्थानत्रयव्यतीतस्य – of the One which is beyond three states; पुनर्जन्मः – rebirth; न – not; विद्यते – is

11. *The Self should be known as One alone in waking, dream and deep sleep. There is no rebirth for the one who goes beyond the three states.*

Truth is that which always is (anvaya). It never gets negated (vyatireka). We can know the Truth or the Self by enquiring, 'What is it that is present all through our experiences in this life and life after life? And what is it that gets negated?'

Each day, all through our lives, we go through the waking, dream and deep sleep states of experiences. All the time we are in either of the three states.

Through the sense organs when we perceive and respond to the gross world outside, we are said to be in the waking state. When the senses fold up and the gross world is not perceived but the mind projects a subtle world within, we experience the dream state. When the senses and the mind both fold up and the gross and subtle world merge into an unmanifest dormant state of experiencing nothing, we are in the deep sleep state. Sometimes we experience in between states like sleepwalking, daydreaming or semi-conscious.

The waking world gets negated in the dream state and the dreamworld in the waking state. Both are absent in the deep sleep state. Hence the three experiences of the waking, dream and deep sleep are not real or the Truth.

Who experiences these three states? Is the waker, dreamer and deep sleeper the same or different? 'I' am awake, 'I' dream and 'I' slept well. The 'I' that is awake alone dreams and sleeps. Who is this 'I' that is common in all the states? It is the 'I thought' (aham vṛtti), the ego (ahaṅkāra) or the individuality (jīvātmā) that owns and experiences the three states. For example, we say 'I am glad to see you in flesh and blood.' 'I dreamt that I was a bird, flying into the heavens!' 'I had an undisturbed and sound sleep in which I knew nothing'. Since the 'I thought', the jīvātmā is present in all our experiences, is it the Truth?

The 'I thought' manifests with each experience and it changes its form with each thought it owns, like 'I am sad', 'I am mad' and so on. It emerges again and again to own each experience. When we enquire into the origin of the 'I thought', it falls and the infinite Truth or the Self that supports and illumines the 'I thought' is realised.[1]

The Truth or the Self is ever-present and is the witness of the three states. It neither emerges or merges nor changes. It is neither a state or a thought, but the very substratum of all states and thoughts.

Who is born and reborn? The 'I thought' or the individual (jīvātmā) identifies with the body and is born as the body. Thus identified, it thinks 'I am a man and so on'. In each life, the jīva identifies with a different body and is born again and again. Only the one who is born can be reborn. The Truth is unborn, and therefore, there is no rebirth for it.

Many get confused when it is said that we are born again and again and that we are birthless. This is because we do not understand the standpoint from which it is said. There is no birth or rebirth for the Truth, but the jīva is born again and again. For example, the water of the ocean is not born, but the waves rise again and again. One who is on earth sees the sun rise and set each day, but for one on the sun, there is no rising and setting.

Therefore one who thinks he is a finite individual (jīva) is born again and again. One who knows he is the infinite Truth is liberated from the cycle of birth and death (punarjanma na vidyate).

---

1 *aham ayaṁ kuto bhavati cinvataḥ, ayi patatyahaṁ nijavicāraṇam.*
ahami nāśabhājyaham-ahaṁtayā, sphurati hṛtsvayaṁ paramapūrṇa sat.
– *Upadeśa-sāraḥ* – 19, 20

The individual (jīvātmā) undergoes the three states of experiences and also birth and rebirth, and the Truth or the Self is its witness. Then are they both not equally real? Is the Truth or the Self in all of us the same? If the Truth or the Self is the witness in each individual, are there not as many truths or selves as there are individuals? The Guru removes these confusions through an example –

Verse 12

एक एव हि भूतात्मा भूते भूते व्यवस्थितः ।
एकधा बहुधा चैव दृश्यते जलचन्द्रवत् ॥ १२ ॥

eka eva hi bhūtātmā bhūte bhūte vyavasthitaḥ,
ekadhā bahudhā caiva dṛśyate jalacandravat. (12)

एक – one; एव – alone; हि – indeed; भूतात्मा – Self in all beings; भूते भूते – in every being; व्यवस्थितः – resident; एकधा – (even though) one alone; बहुधा – as many; च – and; एव – indeed; दृश्यते – is seen; जलचन्द्रवत् – like moon reflected in water

12. *The Self in all beings is one alone, residing in every being. It is seen as one, and as many like the (one) moon reflected in (many) water.*

The full moon shines in all its beauty. The lakes, ponds, rivers, oceans and every other small and big water bodies including tiny droplets, reflect the moon. The reflections are many and varied but the moon is the same, one without a second. Actually the reflections too are the same, but appear different because of the type of water and the size and shape of the container. It appears perfect in pure and still water, unsteady when there are waves and ripples and hazy in muddy water. When the water bodies are dry, there are no reflections, but the moon still shines in all its glory.

Similarly, the Truth is one without a second and the same in all the individuals. The individuals are many and varied. The 'I thought' in each individual is also the same, but the differences are only in the body and mind that the individual identifies with. When the mind is calm, the individual is happy and peaceful and when the mind is agitated, the individual too is disturbed. However with or without the body, mind, individuality or 'I thought', the true Self remains ever shining. It alone is real, the individuality appears and disappears.

The Lord once appeared before Ādi Śaṅkarācārya to remove his delusion. He said, "Is not the sun reflected in the holy river Ganga and the sullied gutters of a slum the same? Can there be any difference in the space enclosed within a gold pot or a mud pot? How can there be this delusion of difference in the Self which is like the waveless Ocean of Bliss, within a holy or cruel man?" [1]

---

[1] *kiṁ gaṅgāmbuni bimbite'mbaramaṇau cāṇḍālavāṭī-payaḥ*
pūre cāntaramasti kāñcanaghaṭī mṛtkumbhayor-vāmbare,
pratyagvastuni nistaraṅga-sahajānandāvabodhāmbudhau
vipro'yaṁ śvapaco'yamityapi mahān ko'yaṁ vibhedabhramaḥ.
– *Manīṣā-pañcakam*-2

The same thought is elaborated upon with another example in the following two verses –

Verse 13 & 14

घटसंवृतमाकाशं नीयमाने घटे यथा।
घटो नीयेत नाकाशः तथा जीवो नभोपमः ॥१३॥

घटवत् विविधाकारं भिद्यमानं पुनः पुनः।
तत् भग्नं न च जानाति स जानाति च नित्यशः ॥१४॥

ghaṭasaṁvṛtam-ākāśaṁ nīyamāne ghaṭe yathā,
ghaṭo nīyeta nākāśaḥ tathā jīvo nabhopamaḥ. (13)

ghaṭavat vividhākāraṁ bhidyamānaṁ punaḥ punaḥ,
tat bhagnaṁ na ca jānāti sa jānāti ca nityaśaḥ. (14)

घटः – pot; संवृतम् – covered; आकाशं – space; नीयमाने घटे – on movement of pot; यथा – just as; घटः – pot; नीयेत – is moved; न आकाशः – not space; तथा – in the same way; जीवः – individual being; नभोपमः – (is) compared with space; घटवत् – like pot; विविधाकारं – various shapes; भिद्यमानं – are broken; पुनः पुनः – again and again; तत् – their; भग्नं – destruction; न – not; च – and; जानाति – knows; सः – He; जानाति – knows; च – and; नित्यशः – always

13. *Just as on movement of pot, the pot (alone) moves and not the space, covered by a pot. In the same way jīva is compared with space.*

14. *Various forms like pot are broken again and again, (yet) the space (in the pot) does not know. But He (the Self, in case of individual bodies) always knows.*

Pots are available in various materials, shapes, sizes and hues, but the space in all of them is the same. We speak of pot space, inside space, outdoor space, open space, outer space, big and small space only with reference to objects. When the auditorium is full, we say there is no space and when sparsely filled we say there is a lot of empty space. However, in the infinite undivided and indivisible space there is no inside or outside, big or small, full or empty.

A pot is moved from place to place or faces east or west. However, space has no direction or motion. When a person is asked to move, we say he made space, but we cannot make or break space.

Just as various concepts and limitations are imposed on space, many limitations and qualities of the body, mind and objects that the individual identifies with are superimposed on the Self like 'I am born', 'I grow', 'I am travelling', 'I am different from you', 'I am better than you'.

Space, like the Self, is infinite space wise, undivided, indivisible, all-pervading, accomodates all and the same in all. Then, is space itself the Self?

Space is a created element. Many objects other than space also exist in space. It is not experienced in the deep sleep state. It is a concept of the mind, inert in nature and known by me. It depends on 'I' for its existence. However, the Self is one without a second, illumines all, is always present, has independent existence and is beyond the mind (sa jānāti ca nityaśaḥ).

One question often asked by spiritual seekers, especially students of Vedānta is, 'How did ignorance start?' The various versions of this question are, 'From when and why did the individual (jīva) start thinking that he is different from the Self?' 'The individual is born again and again. How did the first birth begin?' 'Vāsanās give rise to birth. What was the first vāsanā and how did it start?' 'What comes first the karmas or the bodies, the hen or the chicken?' 'What is born dies. Creation and dissolution follow each other. Which was the first creation? What was its cause?'

After many months of listening to his Guru, Śrī Gurudev again asked Swami Tapovana Mahārāja, "From where did ignorance come?" He was told, "Have you come to seek ignorance or Knowledge? Do not ask how ignorance started. Ask how to end it." Now the Guru shows us how we can remove ignorance –

Verse 15

शब्दमायावृतो नैव तमसा याति पुष्करे ।
भिन्ने तमसि चैकत्वमेक एवानुपश्यति ॥ १५ ॥

śabdamāyāvṛto naiva tamasā yāti puṣkare,
bhinne tamasi caikatvam-eka evānupaśyati. (15)

शब्दमायावृतः – covered by (delusive) power of words; न एव – not at all; तमसा – by (or due to) darkness; याति –

knows; पुष्करे – in the space; भिन्ने – on destruction; तमसि – (of) ignorance; च – and; एकत्वम् – unity; एक – One; एव अनुपश्यति – alone he sees

15. *Due to darkness (ignorance), one does not know the space (the Self) veiled by the word – illusion. On the destruction of darkness (ignorance), one sees the One alone as the unity.*

Māyā or ignorance

Ignorance by itself is not an entity. It is always about something. When we know the thing, our ignorance about it ends. For example, 'I did not know astrophysics. Now I know it well'. Knowledge alone ends ignorance, not action. For example, ignorance of astrophysics cannot be removed by taking a walk.

Similarly, Self-knowledge alone ends ignorance of the Self, not any knowledge like chemistry or action like worship or charity however noble they are. Self-knowledge alone reveals the Self. The Self is known through enquiry about the means of knowledge (pramāṇa vicāra) and the nature of the Truth or the Self (tattva vicāra).

Māyā kārya or the effect of ignorance

Ignorance has two powers. The veiling power (āvaraṇa śakti) veils the Self and the projecting power (vikṣepa śakti) creates a false identity about ourselves and wrong notions about the world like, 'I am the body, the doer of actions' and 'The world is real!' One of the ways that māyā deludes even spiritual seekers is through words.

Śabda śakti or the Power of words

Night covers all with darkness. All differences are hidden and we are unable to perceive anything. Even before sunrise, in the light of dawn, we start seeing and by midday, there is not a trace of darkness or shadow. The world is revealed in all its glory.

The darkness of ignorance veils the Truth and we project many concepts about it. There are many schools of thoughts, religious sects, varied interpretations of scriptures, and different as well as conflicting beliefs about the individual, world and God and their relationship. There is a plethora of written and spoken words, which are like a forest in which a seeker can get easily lost.[1]

Words have an unbelievable power. They can delight or hurt, create friends or enemies, clear doubts or create confusions, make or break relationships, inspire or humiliate, create understanding or misunderstanding and liberate or bind us.

The clouds of words presently cover the pure sky of Self. However, the words of the Guru, self-enquiry and Self-knowledge reveal the one Self which thereafter continues to shine (anupaśyati). The dusk of ignorance never shows its face after the dawn of Self-knowledge.

[1] *śabda-jālaṁ mahāraṇyaṁ citta-bhramaṇa-kāraṇam – Vivekacūḍāmaṇi*-60

Everyone is searching for peace of mind. Now the Guru again recommends the time tested way of gaining lasting peace –

Verse 16

शब्दाक्षरं परं ब्रह्म तस्मिन्क्षीणे यदक्षरम्।
तद्विद्वानक्षरं ध्यायेत् यदीच्छेच्छान्तिमात्मनः ॥ १६ ॥

śabdākṣaraṁ paraṁ brahma tasmin-kṣīṇe yadakṣaram,
tadvidvān-akṣaraṁ dhyāyet yadīcchecchāntim-ātmanaḥ. (16)

शब्दः – sound (Om); **अक्षरं** – word; **परं** – supreme; **ब्रह्म** – Brahman; **तस्मिन्** – in that; **क्षीणे** – disappearance; **यत्** – that which is; **अक्षरम्** – imperishable (is revealed); **तत्** – that; **विद्वान्** – wise one; **अक्षरं** – imperishable; **ध्यायेत्** – should meditate; **यदि** – if; **इच्छेत्** – (he) desires; **शान्तिम्** – peace; **आत्मनः** – of the soul

16. *The sound Om (symbolises) the supreme Brahman. On the disappearance of that (symbol Om), the Imperishable is (revealed). If one desires the peace of the soul, he should meditate on that Imperishable.*

The importance of a thought is reinforced by repetition. The method of meditation propounded in verse seven is again spoken of so that its importance is assimilated.

The Imperishable Letters

The Self is unchanging. The alphabet in Sanskrit is called akṣara-mālā or a garland of letters. Each letter is called akṣara, the imperishable. Letters form words, words form sentences and languages. All knowledge is in the form of languages, be it literature, history or science. Different fields of knowledge may have specific languages like computer language and mathematical formulae, but they also are finally made up of letters. We need to learn to read and write the letters to get initiated into the entire world of knowledge. Words, their meanings, sentences and languages change but the letters and the alphabet remain the same. They are therefore called akṣara, the Imperishable.

The Imperishable Sound

To superimpose an extraordinary feeling or thought on the ordinary and worship it as the extraordinary is the principle behind all worship (upāsanā). The stone is worshipped as a symbol of Śiva and the flag is saluted as a homage to the country. Here on the most sacred sound symbol Om, is superimposed the thought of the Supreme and it is meditated upon as the supreme Self.

The first letter in any alphabet is 'a'. The first sound that emerges from our vocal chords is 'a' (as in but). The last letter of Sanskrit alphabet is 'ma'. The sound that emerges as we close our mouth is 'ma'. All other letters of the Sanskrit alphabet and sound modifications which appear in between 'a' and 'ma' are represented by 'u' (as in put). The sound and the symbol Om made up of the three letters 'a', 'u' and 'm' therefore represent the entire range of sounds, words, meanings, languages, knowledges, the manifest gross and subtle world and the Lord with the universal and particular form, name and qualities (saguṇa Brahma). It also indicates the underlying nameless, formless, attributeless Truth (nirguṇa Brahma) free from all words and sounds. Therefore when we meditate on Om as the Truth, the words and sounds cease and the imperishable silence beyond words and sound is realised as one's own Self. For example, when we hear the words, 'You are the most wonderful person in the world', the meaning is understood and a wonderful feeling arises, in which there are no words.

While chanting and meditating on Om as the imperishable Truth, one leaves all body identification, and attains the supreme Abode.[1]

The Imperishable Silence

It is strange that we all want peace, but we do everything opposed to it. We fight battles, entertain disturbing thoughts, relish conflicts, enjoy horror movies and read violent thrillers.

Some strive to quieten the mind by spiritual practices, control desires, reflect deeply to remove doubts and false notions that cause agitations, and pray fervently for purity and peace of mind. The peace gained through such striving has long lasting effect.

However, everlasting and true peace comes only to one who meditates on the Self. 'How can there be any peace for

---

[1] *omityekākṣaraṁ brahma vyāharan-mām-anusmaran,*
yaḥ prayāti tyajan-dehaṁ sa yāti paramāṁ gatim. – *Gītā*-8.13

the agitated mind?'[1] 'It is they alone who gain lasting peace who meditate and realise the Truth or the Self.'[2]

The Man of Realisation indeed gains the imperishable peace beyond all sounds and words.

1 *na cābhāvayataḥ śāntiḥ aśāntasya kutaḥ sukham* – *Gītā*-2.66

2 *teṣāṁ śāntiḥ śāśvatī netareṣām* – *Kaṭhopaniṣad*-5.13

Does secular knowledge help in realising the Self within? Does the study of the scriptures have any role in attaining the imperishable Truth? The Guru says –

Verse 17

द्वे विद्ये वेदितव्ये तु शब्दब्रह्म परं च यत्।
शब्दब्रह्मणि निष्णातः परं ब्रह्माधिगच्छति ॥१७॥

dve vidye veditavye tu śabdabrahma paraṁ ca yat,
śabdabrahmaṇi niṣṇātaḥ paraṁ brahmādhigacchati. (17)

द्वे – two; विद्ये – knowledge; वेदितव्ये – should be known; तु – indeed; शब्दब्रह्म – word-Brahman (Om); परं – supreme; च यत् – and that (which is); शब्दब्रह्मणि – in word-Brahman; निष्णातः – adept; परं – supreme; ब्रह्म – Brahman; अधिगच्छति – attains

17. *Two knowledges should be known – the word-Brahman (Om) and that which is Supreme. One who is adept in word-Brahman (Om) attains the supreme Brahman.*

The *Muṇḍakopaniṣad* too repeats the thought expressed in this verse – 'two types of knowledges should be known.'[1]

1) **Aparā vidyā or Śabda-Brahma:** It includes –

   a) **Secular knowledge:** Knowledge of the world of objects, things and beings; knowledge studied in modern school

[1] *dve vidye veditavye – Muṇḍakopaniṣad*-1.1.4

and universities; knowledge pursued by researchers in fields like science, economics and politics and all knowledges which are known by us remaining different from them. This also includes the six limbs of the Vedas (vedāṅgas), which are śikṣā (phonetics), kalpa (rituals), vyākaraṇa (grammar), nirukta (etymology), chandas (metres, literature) and jyotiṣa (astrology, astronomy, mathematics)

b) **Scriptural knowledge:** The Vedas, especially the Upaniṣads – also called Vedānta.

c) **Om meditation:** Om represents the Lord with name, form and qualities (saguṇa Brahma), the omniscient and omnipotent Lord who is the creator, sustainer and the destroyer of the universe (Īśvara) or the entire manifest and unmanifest world. Meditation on the sacred Om as the infinite Truth is the highest meditation possible with an external support.

2) **Parā vidyā:** 'It is that knowledge by which the imperishable Truth is realised.'[1] It is the direct means to Realisation (sākṣāt sādhana).

So what is the role of secular knowledge in knowing the Truth? Secular knowledge makes us literate and capable of studying and understanding the scriptures with its various nuances and import.

But what is the need to be well versed in the scriptures? Listening to the scriptures (śravaṇa), study (svādhyāya) and

[1] *yayā tad akṣaram adhigamyate – Muṇḍakopaniṣad*-1.1.5

reflection on the meaning of the scriptures (manana) makes our mind subtle and removes doubts and wrong notions regarding the world and the Self.

One well versed in the scriptures, with a pure, concentrated and subtle mind, meditates on the sacred syllable 'Om' as the Self. The regular practice of such Om meditation exhausts the false notions and impressions of many lifetimes (vāsanā kṣaya) which enables the meditator to directly realise the Self with the supreme Knowledge (parā vidya or para brahma) – 'I am the Imperishable Self' (paraṁ brahma adhigacchati).

In India a child is initiated into the alphabet in a special ceremony called 'akṣara abhyāsa'. The child is first made to inscribe the sacred letter Om, symbolising the imperishable Truth or God or Self . The ultimate purpose of learning the other letters, words, languages and knowledges is in realising the Truth.

But are there not Realised Masters who have not studied the scriptures? Then why is there such emphasis on study of the scriptures?

Verse 18

ग्रन्थमभ्यस्य मेधावी ज्ञानविज्ञानतत्परः ।
पलालमिव धान्यार्थी त्यजेत् ग्रन्थमशेषतः ॥ १८ ॥

grantham-abhyasya medhāvī jñāna-vijñāna-tatparaḥ,
palālam-iva dhānyārthī tyajet grantham-aśeṣataḥ. (18)

ग्रन्थमभ्यस्य – having studied the scriptures; मेधावी – an intelligent student; ज्ञानविज्ञानतत्परः – intent on acquiring knowledge and wisdom; पलालम् – husk; इव – just like; धान्यार्थी – who seeks rice; त्यजेत् – should discard; ग्रन्थमशेषतः – the scriptures altogether

18. *Having studied the scriptures, an intelligent student intent on acquiring knowledge and wisdom should discard the scriptures altogether just like one who seeks rice discards the husk.*

There are number of Realised Masters who have not studied the scriptures. Many scholars got answers to scholastic questions regarding the scriptures, from Śrī Ramana Maharshi, who himself had not studied the scriptures. Paṇḍits have written learned commentaries on simple compositions of great saints like Sūradāsa and Kabīradāsa, who themselves had no formal education. Then why should we read the scriptures? Highly evolved souls like Śrī Ramana Maharshi could have studied the scriptures in a previous birth, the essence of which was carried by them in the next life and which led them to the Truth.[1]

However, mere scholarly study, intellectual discussions, writing commentaries or collecting information about the scriptures cannot lead us to the realisation of the Truth. 'Also an extrovert or indulgent mind cannot understand the subtle essence of the scriptures.'[2] 'The purpose of scriptural studies is to realise the Truth. If that is attained, the study is fruitful, if not it is in vain.'[3]

Swami Vivekananda was once asked what was great about the Vedas. He said, "The Vedas say – study the Vedas and realise the Truth. Then leave the Vedas." In the realisation of the Truth or the Self, the Vedas too stand negated and the Truth alone remains.[4]

Śrī Ādi Śaṅkarācārya urges us to study the scriptures daily[5] and in the *Taittirīya-upaniṣad* in his convocation address to the students the Guru advises them never to be inadvertent in the study and the propagation of the

---

[1] *pūrvābhyāsena tenaiva hriyate hyavaśo'pi saḥ,*
jijñāsurapi yogasya śabdabrahma ativartate – *Bhagavad-gītā*-6.44

[2] *na hi anadhyātmavid jñātuṁ śaknoti vedārthān tattvataḥ*

[3] *avijñāte pare tattve śāstrādhītistu niṣphalā,*
vijñāte'pi pare tattve śāstrādhītistu niṣphalā – *Vivekacūḍāmaṇi*-59

[4] *yatra vedo avedo bhavati* – *Bṛhadāraṇyaka-upaniṣad*

[5] *vedo nityam adhīyatām* – *Sādhanā-pañcakam*-1

scriptures.[1] We are also told to always respect our Guru and scriptures. On the other hand, we are asked to leave the scriptures as one would discard the husk of grains. There seems to be an apparent contradiction.

This confusion arises when we do not understand the distinction between the means and the goal. The scriptures are the means to Self-knowledge. Where is the question of leaving the means, till the goal is reached? Should we abandon the boat till the shore is reached? Once the goal is reached, the means having served their purpose are not required. However, the Realised Master is always grateful to the Guru who taught him the scriptures. He knows that his infinite gain would have been impossible without the Guru and the scriptures, and therefore, he shows great reverence towards them. He truly appreciates the importance of the scriptures, and therefore, he teaches the divine Knowledge enshrined in them to all those who seek it. He may even listen to discourses by other great men on the scriptures or himself read them just to revel in the Truth.[2]

1 *svādhyāya pravacanābhyāṁ na pramaditavyam – Taittirīya-upaniṣad*-I.II.I

2 *vedānta vākyeṣu sadā ramantaḥ – Kaupīna-pañcakam*-1

The scriptures are many. Their statements are varied and seem contradictory. The Masters who propound them are many. Their interpretations are varied and seem contradictory. Thus, will not the study of the scriptures only confuse us further? The Guru now resolves this doubt –

Verse 19

गवामनेकवर्णानां क्षीरस्याप्येकवर्णता ।
क्षीरवत्पश्यते ज्ञानं लिङ्गिनस्तु गवां यथा ॥ १९ ॥

gavām-aneka-varṇānāṁ kṣīrasyāpyeka-varṇatā,
kṣīravat-paśyate jñānaṁ liṅginastu gavāṁ yathā. (19)

गवाम् – cows; अनेकवर्णानां – of multiple colours; क्षीरस्य – of the milk; अपि – while; एकवर्णता – same colour; क्षीरवत् – like milk; पश्यते – sees; ज्ञानं – the Knowledge; लिङ्गिनः – many branched (scriptures); तु – indeed; गवां – cows; यथा – just as

19. *While cows are of different colours, milk is of the same colour. The wise one sees Knowledge like milk while the many branched (scriptures) indeed as cows!*

Unity in diversity:

The word 'go' has many meanings in Sanskrit like cow, earth, speech and Vedas. Cows come in many breeds, sizes and hues. However, all give white milk. The soil and surface of the earth is different in texture, colour and content the world over, yet it nourishes and supports all everywhere. Words vary in meaning and pronunciation but the alphabet of the language is the same. Similarly, the Vedas (scriptures) are many and their statements apparently contradictory, but the knowledge indicated is the same.

The Vedas, especially the Upaniṣads, in some statements clearly reveal the Truth. For example, 'The absolute Truth is of the nature of Existence-Consciousness-Infinite Bliss'[1] and 'That Truth is the Self, That thou art, O Śvetaketo![2]' Such statements are called spaṣṭa liṅga – clear indicators. Many statements which are not that clear are called aspaṣṭa liṅga. The word 'prāṇa' is used in the Vedas to mean the Self, the individual soul, life, the digestive fire, physiological functions or the function of breathing. Such words and statements with different meanings in different contexts could cause confusion.

Different theories of creation are given in different Upaniṣads. In some places, it is said that creation is simultaneous and in the mind of the Lord like a dream. In another place it is said that creation is sequential and elsewhere it is said that there is no creation. Such contradictory statements could also cause confusion.

The great Sage Veda-vyāsa resolved all these apparent differences and contradictions of the mystical statements of the Vedas through the *Brahmasūtras*. He categorically states that the contradictions are only apparent and not

---

1 *satyaṁ jñānam anantaṁ brahma – Taittirīya-upaniṣad*-2.1.1

2 *tat-satyaṁ sa ātmā tat-tvam-asi śvetaketo – Chāndogya-upaniṣad*-6.8.7

real. The purpose of the entire Vedas is in indicating the same Truth.[1]

Knowledge is true to the object of knowledge and not the knower. Therefore right knowledge is to know a thing 'as it is' and not according to the interpretation or subjective opinion of the knower. Therefore even though Realised Masters may come from different backgrounds and may have followed different paths, but their experience of Realisation or knowledge of the Truth is the same. The Nirvāṇa of a Gautama Buddha is the same as the 'mokṣa' of a Swami Vivekananda.

---

[1] *tattu samanvayāt – Brahmasūtra*-4

Even after listening to the Guru and the scriptures we are unable to 'see' the Truth. Why is that so? What process will make this knowledge our own direct experience? The following two verses explain the role of reflection and enquiry through two different examples –

Verse 20 & 21

घृतमिव पयसि निगूढं भूते भूते वसति विज्ञानम् ।
सततं मन्थयितव्यं मनसा मन्थानभूतेन ॥ २० ॥

ज्ञाननेत्रं समादाय उद्धरेत् वह्निवत्परम् ।
निष्कलं निश्चलं शान्तं तद्ब्रह्माहमिति स्मृतम् ॥ २१ ॥

ghṛtamiva payasi nigūḍhaṁ bhūte bhūte vasati vijñānam,
satataṁ manthayitavyaṁ manasā manthānabhūtena. (20)

jñānanetraṁ samādāya uddharet vahnivatparam,
niṣkalaṁ niścalaṁ śāntaṁ tadbrahmāhamiti smṛtam. (21)

घृतम् – butter; इव – just like; पयसि – in milk; निगूढं – is hidden; भूते भूते – in every being; वसति – resides; विज्ञानम् – awareness; सततं – constantly; मन्थयितव्यं – should churn; मनसा – by mind; मन्थानभूतेन – by the churning rod; ज्ञाननेत्रं – rope of knowledge; समादाय – having taken; उद्धरेत् – one should bring out; वह्निवत् – like fire; परम् – Supreme (Brahman); निष्कलं – partless; निश्चलं – immutable; शान्तं – peaceful; तत् – that; ब्रह्म – Brahman; अहम् – I am; इति – thus; स्मृतम् – is thought of

20. *Just like butter is hidden in the milk, awareness resides in every being. To discover that, one should constantly churn with the mind as the churning rod.*

21. *One should bring out the Supreme (Brahman) like fire, by taking the rope of knowledge (to churn the mind). 'I am that Brahman (which is) immutable, peaceful and without parts' – is thought of (by the Realised seers).*

The process of making clarified butter (ghṛtam) prevailed even in the Vaidika times. The Guru first gives an example which was familiar to all in India till even half a century ago. A spoonful of yeast culture was mixed with warm milk and allowed to mature overnight. The curd (yogurt) formed was thereafter mixed with water and churned with a churning rod to separate the butter from the buttermilk. The butter was heated till it became clarified butter which was then used for cooking, lighting lamps or as an offering in the sacrificial fire.

Butter is always present in every drop of the milk even though not seen in the milk. It only needs a special process to manifest it. Similarly, the Truth is present in all beings as the infinite Self – right from an ant to the divine Creator of each cosmos.[1] Yet we are unable to experience it. The best of student realises the Truth by ascertaining its nature just by listening to the Guru.[2] However, most even when taught are unable to realise the Self. The process of churning – constant and independent reflection (manana) is needed to bring out the essence of the teaching and realise it.

[1] *yā brahmādi-pipīlikānta tanuṣu protā jagatsākṣiṇī – Manīṣā-pañcakam*-1

[2] *tattva niścaya mātreṇa prājño bhavati dhīmatām.*

For example, the Guru says, "I am not the body". But everyone, from my childhood onwards, has always interacted with me as the body, so I must be the body. Everyone cannot be wrong. But can I be this ever-changing body made up of cells that regularly perishes? I am still here, even though the cells that constituted my body a few years back are dead and gone, and those that are now part of the body shall die sooner or later. I cannot possibly be the body. By such reflection we independently arrive at the same knowledge that the Guru gives us. Such ascertained and doubtless knowledge can then be meditated upon (nididhyāsana) and realised.

Right from the Vaidika age the fire used for all rituals was kindled with a special instrument. Two wooden cups were rotated in the opposite direction with the help of a churning rod and a rope. The friction created sparks which were tended by cotton to produce fire. This example illustrates the process of enquiry.

The mind like the churning rod is churned with the rope of enquiry. The words of the Guru and our own doubts and experiences are reflected upon to create the fire of Self-knowledge which burns away the deadwood of ignorance, vāsanās and wrong notions. For example, the thought that 'I am the part of the whole' is burnt away in the knowledge 'I am the partless whole' through the enquiry – 'who am I?'

The Upaniṣad ends with the following verse –

Verse 22

सर्वभूताधिवासं यत् भूतेषु च वसत्यपि ।
सर्वानुग्राहकत्वेन तदस्म्यहं वासुदेवः
तदस्म्यहं वासुदेव इति ॥२२ ॥

sarvabhūtādhivāsaṁ yat bhūteṣu ca vasatyapi,
sarvānugrāhakatvena tadasmyahaṁ vāsudevaḥ
tadasmyahaṁ vāsudeva iti. (22)

सर्वभूताधिवासं – abode of all beings; यत् – that which; भूतेषु – in all beings; वसति – lives; च अपि – and also; सर्व – all; अनुग्राहकत्वेन – by being gracious; तत् – that; अस्मि अहं – I am; वासुदेवः – one residing in all; तत् – that; अस्मि अहं – I am; वासुदेवः – one residing in all; इति – thus

22. *I am That one which is the abode of all beings and also who lives in all beings by being gracious to all. I am that Vāsudeva – one residing in all, I am that Vāsudeva – one residing in all.*

'Vas' means 'to live or exist'. 'adhivāsa' means a residence or abode.

The Abode of all beings (sarva-bhūta-adhivāsaṁ)

Where do we all reside? In what do we exist? All things and beings exist in time and space. But what do time and space exist in? The whole world 'was', 'is' and 'will be'. All beings that 'were', 'are' and 'will be' exist in and because of the principle of Existence. Without existence nothing would exist – neither time, space or objects. Existence alone is the true abode of all things and beings.

Lives in all beings (bhūteṣu ca vasati api)

All exist in one Existence, but is there one entity that exists in all? The world including my body exists in my mind. My mind exists in 'I' and is centred in 'I' alone even though it keeps running from object to object. Hence the 'Self' alone exists in all beings. That 'Self' has to be of the nature of existence which is common in all beings. Hence I, as the pure Self, am the Existence in all beings.

As the bestower of grace (anugrāhakatvena)

Do we not consider it grace of another when our very existence depends on them? Do we not feel blessed by one who gives and sustains our life? The Truth which is of the very nature of existence, blesses all by giving existence and life to all. A dead body has no beauty or talent. Without the Life Principle, it is considered inauspicious and either buried or burnt. Blessed indeed is our very existence and our life because of the Truth in us. To know that we are thus blessed is itself a great blessing!

That Vāsudeva I am (tadasmi ahaṁ vāsudevaḥ)

Anything other than Existence is non-existent and other than Consciousness – the Knowledge Principle, is inert. Existence being eternal and unchanging can never be inert and

Consciousness being the knower cannot ever become non-existent. Therefore Existence (vāsu) alone is Consciousness (deva). I am of the nature of Existence-Consciousness (Vāsudeva).

There existed a king by the name of Pauṇḍraka who started thinking that he was the real Vāsudeva Kṛṣṇa and that the Lord, the King of Dwaraka was an imposter who called himself Vāsudeva Kṛṣṇa. He would imitate the Lord in all his ways and mannerisms and boast about his achievements. The Lord went to him and killed him in battle. Pauṇḍraka became one with the Lord. Pauṇḍraka symbolises a seeker. A seeker starts meditating, 'I am Vāsudeva (Existence-Consciousness)'. His attempts feel like vain imitations of the Truth and seem almost a boast. How can I, a finite individual be the infinite Vāsudeva? However, by the grace of God and Guru and his own consistent efforts his finite identity is destroyed and he realises, 'I am truly Vāsudeva of the nature of Existence-Consciousness'.

The Upaniṣad ends with the repetition of the words 'That Vāsudeva I am, That Vāsudeva I am'. It signifies the doubtless ascertainment of the Truth directly experienced on Realisation, respect for this sacred knowledge and the end of the teaching and text.

The Upaniṣad began with the categorisation of the mind as impure and pure and analysing its role in causing bondage and Liberation. On enquiry into its true nature, the problems of the mind resolve and the mind dissolves and the Truth is realised as 'all is Vāsudeva, the infinite

Self within'. One who realises thus is indeed very rare and great.[1]

O Vāsudeva! Salutation to you. All these worlds (three) are liveable only because you exist there. In fact you are the abode of all beings, also you live in them as their true Self.[2]

With the direct realisation of this immortal Knowledge and the grace of the Guru and God may we too attain immortality.

Om Tat Sat

[1] *vāsudevaḥ sarvamiti sa mahātmā sudurlabhaḥ – Bhagavad-gītā*-7.19

[2] *vāsanād vāsudevasya vāsitaṁ bhuvana-trayam,*
sarva-bhūta-nivāso'si vāsudeva namo'stu te.
– *Viṣṇu-sahasranāma* phalaśruti